# DINOSAURS

# Now YOU can read about . . .

# DINOSAURS

ORIGINAL TEXT BY HARRY STANTON

REVISIONS BY WILLOWISP PRESS INC.

ILLUSTRATED BY BOB HERSEY

BRIMAX BOOKS • NEWMARKET • ENGLAND

Dinosaur means "terrible lizard." Dinosaurs were the largest animals to have walked on the earth. The largest dinosaurs weighed up to fifty tons and were about twenty-five meters (81 feet) long.

No one has ever
seen a dinosaur.
Dinosaurs died out
long before there
were any men or
women on the earth.

Each Brontosaurus dinosaur weighed as much as six elephants. Brontosaurus stayed together in herds because they were attacked by meat-eating dinosaurs.

Brontosaurus
(*bron-toe-SAW-rus*)

The largest dinosaur was the Diplodocus. It was as long as three school buses. It was able to raise its head very high so that it could eat leaves from the tops of trees.

Diplodocus
(*dih-PLOD-o-cus*)

Dinosaurs that did not eat plants were meat-eating dinosaurs. They ate other dinosaurs.

Tyrannosaurus Rex
(*tie-ran-o-SAW-rus rex*)

The Tyrannosaurus Rex was the largest of the meat-eating dinosaurs. It stood on its back legs and was over six meters (20 feet) high. It weighed eight tons. Tyrannosaurus Rex had long sharp teeth and very short arms.

Many plant-eating dinosaurs ran away when they were attacked. But some who moved slowly had armor.

Stegosaurus was as long as a bus. On its back it had two rows of bony plates for armor. There were no plates on its sides to protect it.

Stegosaurus
(*steg-o-SAW-rus*)

Ankylosaurus
(*an-kile-o-SAW-rus*)

The flat back of the
Ankylosaurus was covered in
armor. Look at the bony
club at the end of its tail.
The club could be used if
the Ankylosaurus had to
fight other dinosaurs.

These strange bone-headed
dinosaurs had very thick
skulls. The bone of their skulls
was over twenty-five centimeters
(10 inches) thick. Their thick skulls
protected these dinosaurs when they fought.

Look at the long horn which the Parasaurolophus had on the back of their heads. They ate leaves with jaws that looked like a duck's beak. Inside their jaws were hundreds of small sharp teeth. When their teeth wore down they grew new ones.

Parasaurolophus
(pa-ra-saw-ROL-o-fuss)

Triceratops
(*try-SER-a-tops*)

The Triceratops had three very long horns, one on its nose and one over each eye. Covering its neck was a shield of bone. Triceratops had flat teeth to help it eat tough leaves.

Another horned dinosaur was the Styracosaurus. It had a horn on its nose seventy centimeters (28 inches) long. Its head was over two meters (6 feet) long. The dinosaur weighed three and one-half tons.

Styracosaurus
(*sty-rak-o-SAW-rus*)

Horned dinosaurs ate plants. They used their sharp horns to charge any other dinosaurs that attacked them.

At the same time as the dinosaurs, strange creatures hunted in the sea. Ichthyosaurus means "fish lizard." It had sharp teeth and large eyes.

Plesiosaurs were about twelve meters (39 feet) long. They had large flat flippers and very long necks.

Plesiosaur
(*PLES-e-o-sawr*)

Ichthyosaurus
(*ik-thee-o-SAW-rus*)

Pterosaur
(*TER-o-sawr*)

Strange-looking creatures flew in the air. Winged lizards, called Pterosaurs, had skin between their long front feet and their short back legs. The largest was twelve meters (39 feet) from wing tip to wing tip. Others were only as big as robins.

The age of dinosaurs came to an end.
All the dinosaurs died out when the
earth became cooler about sixty-five
million years ago. This did not happen
suddenly. It took thousands of years.

Perhaps the earth became too cold for dinosaurs to live. Perhaps they did not have enough food.

Even the strange creatures that flew in the air, and those that swam in the sea, died out.

The bones of some
dinosaurs can still be
found today. When
some of the creatures
died they fell into
soft mud. This mud
gradually hardened.
The bones then
became fossils and
the mud around them
hardened into rock.

Some fossils are
found when the rock is
worn away. Other
fossils are found in
mines or stone
quarries.

# What are the names of these dinosaurs?

Ankylosaurus

Bone-headed
Dinosaur

Brontosaurus

Diplodocus

Ichthyosaurus

Parasaurolophus

Plesiosaur

Pterosaur

Stegosaurus

Styracosaurus

Triceratops

Tyrannosaurus
Rex